GOLD

GEORGE ELLIOTT CLARKE

GASPEREAU PRESS
Printers & Publishers
2016

Beauty ... is the sole business of poetry.
ROBINSON JEFFERS, "THE BEAUTY OF THINGS"

Na kelu'lk we'jitu (I find Beauty).
RITA JOE, "ANKITA'SI (I THINK)"

For Geraldine Elizabeth Clarke (1939–2000)
& William Lloyd Clarke (1935–2005)

Adepts, Believers, African Baptists

GOLD BAR

What is here?
Gold? Yellow, glittering, precious gold?
WILLIAM SHAKESPEARE, *TIMON OF ATHENS*

Gold only heals
Ills that aren't ills.
X. STATES

My previous "colouring books," namely *Blue* (2001, 2011, 2014), *Black* (2006, 2012), and *Red* (2011), were attempts to, in part, write outside lines and connect moving dots. Now, here is *Gold*, a colour I carry in my skin, even if I am not, alas, formed of such mettle.

1 *NISAN* MMXVI   GEORGE ELLIOTT CLARKE (X. STATES)

GOLD MINE

Money : Joke
could be wiped out
…
and was when
gold and pound were
devalued
WILLIAM CARLOS WILLIAMS, *PATERSON*

Anatomies	15	Gold Foil
Poetics	25	Gold Coin
Politics	49	Gold Star
Sapphics	75	Gold Heart
Eclogues	93	Gold Leaf
The Six	115	Gold Coast
Epigrams	137	Gold Medal
Notes	141	Gold Record
Acknowledgements	147	Gold Watch
An Alphabetic List of Poem Titles	153	Gold Rush

GOLD FOIL

This man lived gold, thought gold, dreamed gold.
IAN FLEMING, *GOLDFINGER*

Compound Interest
VENICE, APRIL 2010

Duplicity

Two-faced poet? That's me.* "Guilty"—as framed.
My double visage suits my double tongue—
Spieling out twice-told tales in spliced duets—
Paper-and-ink, print-on-a-screen—unless
I redouble lies by dubbing aloud.
     Let's say my art's "Romantic," so I sport
A rosy halo—like printers' devils,
And blaze all night, steeped in *rosé* or blush
(Bed)sheets.... Or say I'm extra "*noir*," extra
"*Polar*," my face pairing disappeared heart—
AWOL, paroled, sentenced no more to *Love*....
Or say my background's orange—a hint of sun:
It gilds "Apollo"; suns appalling *Guilt*.
     This triptych of twin selves tells I'm split—
North, South, East, West, Hyde-and-Jekyll; thus, each
Ensemble dissembles—in resembling me.

---

* Cf. portraits by Marco Cera, Guy D. Andrea, *et al.*, unveiled in April 2014 at the Art Gallery of Ontario (courtesy of a class in portraiture taught by Aleks Bartosik).

Golden Moments

Gold is *il vino dei poeti* on a Lufthansa flight bridging Longfellow and Dante*

Gold is the gleaming chaos of Venetian canals, emerald as Portuguese wine

Gold is gusts of *Grief* from lousy lungs, wallowing in sallow phlegm

Gold is bottomless *Depravity* and overthrown *Virginity*

Gold is perfume hissing from a white lady, black hair kissing her thighs

Gold is tireless light, ageless light, endlessly embryonic light, ignited darkness, as in The Bahamas

Gold is *Love*: Spread-eagled *L* and *v*; and *o*, so violated, it looks like *e*

Gold is the Red Army sacking Berlin and Black Shirts ransacking Rome

Gold is blue-collar rapists and white-collar pedophiles

Gold is using your face, your ass, to flush out coffee and cream

Gold is delirious ebony, whalebone-corseted in merchant's ivory

Gold is red wine bleeding through the skin of a tablecloth

Gold is *The Merchant of Venice*, *Timon of Athens*, and *The Merry Wives of Windsor*: A swingers' club

Gold is a dove, its throat cut, gory moonlight spewing free

Gold is burnt sienna, umber periwinkle, cerulean charcoal

Gold is a whore by nature and a prostitute by profession

Gold is Malcolm X, Iceberg Slim, Miles Davis, and Dorothy Proctor-Mills

Gold is "never having to say I'm sorry"

Gold is *Goldfinger*, *Diamonds Are Forever*, and *The Man with the Golden Gun*

Gold is neutrally lurid, brutally metaphysical

Gold is the Writers' Centre of Madeira rebranded as The School of Criminology

---

* Cf. Karin.

Gold is an unyielding, unrehearsed, unexpected truth
Gold is Bellini *bianco blanc* apple vermouth (sold by Loblaws in
    Gatineau-Hull)
Gold is Marx & Lenin, Lennon & McCartney, Mao and dirty linen
Gold is *Tim Tam Tum*, the coffee-dark wine that sticks like caramel
Gold is the sugar-maple Burns of Nova Scotian chainsaw poets
Gold is Andorra, Monte Carlo, Malta, Rodos, Barbados, and
    rainbows between
Gold is Maurice *Calvados* Sachs *Calvados* Violette *Calvados*
    Leduc—that triangle
Gold is a black Lolita nymphet who's palimpsest to a white Laila
    elderessa*
Gold is extinguished purple and distinguished silver and
    anguished grey
Gold is the sun lost in the shade of the moon
Gold is *Directions Home* and *Traverse*; *Illicit Sonnets* and *Extra
    Illicit Sonnets*:
Fool's gold and sulphur; sunlight and the philosopher's stone
Gold is *Gold*—the light before your eyes.

---

* Cf. "Lil Bear."

Welcoming The Year of the Fire-Red Monkey

    (*pace* Taeho Han)

Fragile, shining, icicle webs dangle—
    white as Hollywood pin-ups....
Shaky, they can be wind-shattered,
    battered down,
assemble broken mementoes
    of winter's *Sovereignty*.

Under the canopy of the calendar—
    its squared and hollow days
(each more or less the same,
    if minutely longer or shorter),
we creep at each other like tarantulas—
    surgical, deliberate, tender—
our limbs merging as if hungry,
    or indiscriminate.

Why can't we mimic expansive aromas—
    and be attached, but not parasitic?
Why can't we be as vital as the blood
    purring and booming,
entombed within us,
    but surging and thrusting like roots?

Let's not squabble over quibbles
    anymore,
but liberate our long nights
    with short stories,
or bury our dead atop mountains,
    glacial faces upturned to stars.

Music best replenishes *Loss*,
    for it enlists heart, brain, soul,
in the prayer of *Existence*,
    ephemeral and eternal,
what keeps *Time*
    and what is timeless.

May I give myself *Solace*?
    Too soon has come the moment
when I can say,
    "I last saw my father alive then;
I last saw my mother alive there;"
    and soon arrives the moment
when I will say,
    "I last saw Hamlet played then;
I last heard 'Pass Me Not' there."
    One day I'll realize that never again'll
I witness the tragedy or audit the spiritual,
    that *Art* is all *Memory*.

The calendar is perpetual *Dream*
    and *Memory*,
prayer and loss.
    The frost without mandates fire within.
But I have no logs,
    and no wood to cut.

The early winter leaves grass brown-green;
    the shed leaves dye black-brown.
All my inklings of tomorrow
    are clouds.

True: Saviours flock, promising
	savings, triumphs at gambling,
conquests—prickings—of frozen ladies.
	They all have pin-stripe shoulders
and fat thighs,
	and are glossy with oils,
if not sweat,
	and carry tattered, ratty I.D.

At times, these Saviours petrify me,
	for they go on killing sprees—
backing one mute god or another—
	and I wish they'd sink back
into their caves
	of newsprint and ticker-tape,
where they plot bankruptcies and beheadings.
	Their religions are rank pulp fictions:
coitus-reek,
	gore-stench.

When I heed the news, I should sweat.
	It tears my eyes; it pricks my ears—
to attend the vision of piled-up dead
	and hear their final moans;
their *Despair* that we never refrain
	from starting wars for the same reasons
as always.
	Memorials support armorials.

The good news? Spring will start, upstart,
	in nine-and-a-half weeks.

Also, the wooden bed where we sport
    amorously is evergreen,
a stand-up *Philosophy*
    arises with my sap.

On my table, we have pears—
    cut pears and canned pears.
They are dull suns, a tinny gold,
    but fleshy and tasty—
like the likely milky innards of breasts.
    The pears are as exotic
as oranges and tangerines,
    but are also winsome, homely,
though not aromatic.
    Also, they're not expensive,
which is a godsend, for, today,
    the stock market tanked by 10%
again, due to New Year's frauds
    gobbling last year's profits.

Let us pray against *Alienation*,
    grave-dirt, frigid temperatures,
and any further exile,
    so that April seems divine.

(*Hedonism* is a healthy escape
    from *Atheism's* pessimism.)

Turn the new page, the new leaf!
    A sharp April wind lunges and cleanses.

GOLD COIN

Poetry or gold? / What will it be?
SALIMAH VALIANI, "POETRY OR GOLD"

Hostile Witness
LISBON, MARCH 2009

Introduction: 'On Paths Known to No One'

The melancholy beauty of Cosma's poetry is
Black sunlight, burgundy intoxication,
A Chinese tranquility:
Happiness never outpaces *Sorrow* for long....

Tears? She sees them as Tiffany crystal
Melted down to hot-blooded snow.
In her mind, *Love* sneers at valentines:
It just doesn't suit pretty words.

Her hurtful *Art* screams out *Truth* at birth:
The lover sleeps with the beloved,
But yearns for a hot-lipped vampire.
Desire is *Despair*.

God is opaque, says Cosma. *Evil* is lucid.
Eden hosts angels—and maggots.
What heart ain't wholly rotten?
The holy is so unnatural.

Fairy tales are as merciless as *Scripture*:
That's the secret of both.
Cosma knows it, and so traces Dickinson,
But a Dickinson seduced by Plath.

So Cosma's lyrics well up from desert oases—
Distance—in Greece, Argentina, America—
Empires of myth, mirage, and murder.
Cavafy, praying, meets Neruda, singing.

Cosma is as diligent as *Hunger*:
Even though our maps omit Paradise,
Her vision pushes us into light,
But light, as she shows, having the consistency of shadow.

Upon Reading Flavia Cosma's 'Thus Spoke the Sea'

I.

Like theologians of flames and bones,
We all read *Literature* badly:
We think it is cabalistic *Scripture*,
For we have heard it moaning, dying,
In a professor's suffocating briefcase:
All the love poems shrivelling into epitaphs.

  We league together and laugh out loud:
"Here is another poem that doesn't quite work.
See: The light it should bring is broken like water."
We diagnose the diseased morals,
The Vichy-vicious visions
Of politically noxious bards,
And all their fossil, fussed over *Poesy*,
Whose lines, once elastic with *Music*,
Are long gone crusty, clunky, leaden,
And decayed into dissertations—
To hobble *bel canto* with cant—
Contraband balderdash….

(They claimed they were making *Art*,
But their clamour became hard to make out.)

  Espy all those rickety typists at old typewriters!
Those maimed, vengeful creatures,
Whose *Grace* is pure sludge:
May we credit their heart-felt plagiarisms
With a hitherto, neglected *Excellence*?
Cops alone decipher and then dissect their texts—
Each accurate sham,
Each purveyor of perverted *Originality*:

Dilapidated syllables,
Clacking critiques,
Drugged murmurs.

    Witness: The Canuck poets who are dead,
The damnable British poets,
And the vulgar Yankee poets
Say nothing—
Only their mistakes are beautiful.

    II.

The sun brands us with its *History*—
As resistless and as scarring as lava:
Drowsy, crumbling *Grammar*,
An airless language best printed as equations,
Plus bloated dictionaries,
Suppurating with uselessly ambiguous worms.

We can't be blamed for thinking,
"Throat slit, skull smashed in: The Muse is finished.
Comatose, the outdated heretic
Gasps on in *Folklore*, ransacked diaries—
The repercussions of singing."

    We wonder, "Was it Verlaine who injected Rimbaud with
        ague,
Causing that ultimate priest to shimmer, finally,
As shameless and as gaudy as a saviour?"

Well, throw face-down all those used books.
A poet is only useful as a poet.

III.

Ink is smoky water—scribbler liquor—
Unless we apply the tyrannical discipline of *Beauty*,
To paint *Pain* in thoroughly painful words,
So *Language* cracks like lightning.
In true poetry, ink must bleed.

Our *Satisfaction* is faction—
Violent song and perfidious, savage lungs—
Not confection, not mere *Fiction*.

Ogle insect jewels sparkling in fruit pulp and juice—
Mimicking Sade partisans screwing in rooms
Maggoted by shadows, some crude, boisterous,
The libertine sun blithely urging them on:
Like those vitiated virgins, copulating,
And furious with liquor—the poet
Indulges her culture, sucks its nectar,
Luxuriates, riots lushly, in *Rot*,
Wasting everything to glittering *Waste*,
To strew her hosts with gems divined from garbage.

IV.

Attend, thus, Flavia Cosma—
Too earthy for atmospherics,
Too ethereal for prisons:
She maps Eden as a bestial Utopia.

Her words revive Ovid—but in "Canuckistan" English:
See Ovid with a halo of wasps.

Inspect herein a different slant to the line:
Emily Dickinson donning Sylvia Plath's Siberian persona

(Or *vice versa*),
Or the Québécois poet, Marie Uguay,
Angel Frankensteined-to-life amid gold gloom—
I mean, this iridescent, irredentist Arctic illumination.

No yatterer or yammerer,
No *Occult* cultivator,
Cosma produces a scrupulous *Surrealism*,
Fairy-tales that bite and embitter *Kindergarten* inmates....

Every *Dream* has its sly haunting—
Fears intolerably sexual,
Desires unnaturally animal,
Such lucid make-believe....

So Cosma's poetry yields buried *Music*,
Cheery *Debauchery*, infamous blood,
Tinsel crucifixes, stale-dated *Gospel*,
Cankered wine, mutilated bread,
Bookish stains, zero-worry, sub-zero *Love*,
Rhinestone phantoms, upstart shades and stars,
The rotting of papal balconies,
And rust lingering on into August corn.

Her lines quake the brain like an authentic *Sazerac* cocktail
(Ruthless, New Orleans concoction
Of bourbon, brandy, and caustic caramel),
Or maybe like Romania's infernal *Țuică* grappa—
Clear lyric—
Generic, organic....

Here is *Light* archetypal—
Lustre atypical.

Austin C. Clarke's "When He Was Free and Young and He Used to Wear Silks" (1971): Subtext

I.

Navigating the archipelago of rainbow lips
    and neon-lustrous nylons,
plus islands of pepper in the Caesar,
    the reefs of lime in the Cuba libre,
and dodging the chiseled, Aztec, bas-relief
    of *Cruelty* ebon Shebas profile—
their chatter always as indecipherable
    as Papal Latin,
swished suave I into the Pilot Tavern—
    me garbed as for Tiger's Coconut Grove
(at Kensington Market), but now
    stepping off Bloor into Yorkville
(5th Avenue gone Greenwich Village),
    under an August moon as lemony
as that unmoored by the untaught Rousseau,
    but projecting wishes as dreamy
as the philosophy of the other Rousseau—
    came this black-ink scribe to escape
the chop-chop guillotines of cops' mouths,
    the manacles of critics' eyeglasses,
the dismembering megaphones
    of Dixieland *Kitsch* jazz
(the engrained dirt in *Wonder*-white-*Bread*,
    ad-jingle-crammed, T.O. ears),
and the unspoiled fists of Black Panther imports,
    kept tight-leashed by Brampton Billy's thugs—
and so boogied down I to chant Rastafarian,
    Ah, frumoasă! Frumoasă!—
Ah, beautiful! Beautiful!—
    because the Pilot Tavern is Toronto's Parthenon

(at least for tonight),
    and the silk patina of my *Bombay Sapphire*
gin martini (with three olives),
    hid from *Inhibition*,
the subversive *Geometry* of sable breasts
    or ladies' angular, flexible legs,
one black woman's stretched out leg
    lecherous gainst mine,
under a table sized to fit only two glasses,
    so that the poetry of my Negroni cocktail
outshouted and outvoted
    all that short-pants, childish, Anglican theology,
all that incense that ferries the aroma
    of young corpses
or of kiddies cored and/or buggered
    in the warrens of His and Her Majesties' churches....

II.

"Haii, Clarke," the slinky, leggy lady exhaled,
    and her breath came as fresh in my direction
as one of Bridgetown's April sea breezes,
    though she had the green-apple-sour look
of a just-bitten-into virgin,
    her *Innocence* gone cracked, but juicy,
and juicy, but tart—
    as if her Romeo were gnawing her
like a badly starved stallion.....
    Despite the mahogany summer,
the sable, sultry evening,
    the bluish liquor in the single, divorcée's glass,
the blush of orange lipstick at the lip,

        the skin-tight sheen of her gilt-flecked nylons
making *Goldschläger*-mint chocolates of her legs,
        I also espied her Song-of-Solomon *Elegance*,
her coy, mischievous peeping at her rivals
        (whether masculine or feminine);
her gleaming, statue demeanour,
        which meant that a tear would freeze
if ever one tried to cross her face;
        her tart, soldierly temperament
that declared her no longer married,
        no longer burdened, but free,
and newly single, but "experienced" in bed;
        no longer naïve at what comes naturally,
and at ease with herself, her conscience,
        her conscious science when at *Pleasure*;
and at ease with her long-gone history—
        the former frenzy of *Adultery*,
given her acid-bath-baptism
        in the healing balm of *Feminism*,
just a comin-on-strong now,
        and affording gotten-with-it women,
even wives,
        the dirty *Privilege*
of fucking come who may,
        so that *Coitus* issues humid *Ecstasy*,
just a so-trusty-it's-rusty *Strategy*
        to ditch a dude
before he ditches you
        or ditches your heart,
leaving *une femme* to suffer
        squalid, senescent *Solitude*,
of come-dawn-*Abandonment*....

III.

"Haii, Clarke!" The *belle dame* divorcée
purred with pertinent glances,
    her Rich-Dead-Nazi air
(exhaling *Goldschläger*, *Jägermeister*,
        and peppermint schnapps in equal thirds)
haloing and uplifting her
    above the Pilot Tavern's *ce soir* set
of squalid, snail-textured, slimy winks
    of lounge bunnies and bar-stool toms
(all squarely, unrepentantly lewd),
    their scandalous impulses
and principles of Shakespearean *Bastardy*
    (as if Romeo were Caliban
and Juliet was Lady Macbeth).
    But I knew I shouldn't mistake
this ex-wife's sexual *Laxity* as *Caprice*,
    for lovemaking *Serendipity*
isn't capriciousness,
    just as Serendip isn't Capri:
The two islands sit in different seas.
    My Negroni was a fickle refuge—
or a glossy weakness—
    while I offered the onyx madame
cigarette-smoke-pallid compliments
    that only metastatized her malignant *Ego*,
so that it became my foggy hope
    that she'd name her fave pagan as Priapus
and become my handy Venus,
    or agree that *Romance* is garbage,
topped off with the ice cream that's *Sex*,
    and that it's better to go straight
to the ice cream,

>   rather than amble through the trashy preamble,
> for the mechanics of *Intercourse*
>   seldom involve gregariously engineered *Commerce*,
> even if authentically unprincipled
>   and ideologically louche,
> but are, rather, spasmodic joints
>   and plumbing
> that render he-and-she supernatural, divine,
>   despite the underlying, undying *Sleaze*.
> (*And wasn't this sweet bitch worth every sweet scent?*)
>   I ordered us both, both tequila
> and Champagne, to knock out
>   two knock-out "Chaquilas,"
> to benefit the ex-wife *panochita*
>   with her Las Vegas Strip, *Fredericks-of-Hollywood* bust,
> the *Playboy*-inspired *Playtex* that presented
>   two dark velvet breasts
> as two maracas, already shaking,
>   stirring. Airy manners were kaput.
> *Will she or won't she?* That's what mattered—
>   the diesel promise of Jack-diving-into-the-box
> and uncramped, capacious *Vice*,
>   the woman's vampire grin as she slurps
> the vicarious milk I pump,
>   while I mumble plumped-up, plunked-down words
> at her haggard chugging
>   of my spit-polished spigot,
> and then we spur on *Pomp* and *Circumstance*
>   in an earthy bed,
> romping, raunchy, rambunctious,
>   until thrills roll up and down her spine,
> and we enjoy clustered eruptions....

She rose; *Nature* called.
I schemed a booty call; I watched
    her sumptuous *gluteus maximus* wine*
as she went, her model skin tone
    shimmering a coffee splendor.
Will we be practiced playmates? I wondered.

IV.

    The waiter levitates armfuls of bottles,
ditches them at each table,
    one by one by one,
like a deconstructive Noah.
    A two-tongued Torontonian,
part-Cabbage-Town and part-Rosedale,
    now annexed by U of T classes
and a cockroach and rattail apartment,
    doing nightclub waiting
as his part-time-prison vacation,
    the lad finally reached me,
whose tongue was gutting the sediments
    sentimental at the base
of my glassy, basic instincts. Still,
    my hands spoke the rustling,
Moloch lingo of moolah—
    to bring on more booze—
more psychological gasoline—
    so that the singular divorcée splits—
James Brown-like—her inner thighs,
    to show a pink flourish,
the dawn of sunny *Debauchery*,

---

* Cf. Trinidadian English.

after offing her short-lived lingerie.
The feministized *divorcée* returned.
My lungs changed chords.
Preening amid smoke and Smoky Robinson—
　　his meddling, wah-wah cries,
this independent woman surveyed, for me,
　　the Eliotic *Waste Land* that's *Divorce*,
while I spilled down precious fluids
　　in unbroken ripples,
and the lady sucked sexily at her drinks,
　　secreting, now and then,
the gaseous piss of a pregnant silence.
　　I eyed the other patrons—
men—jolly, plush, gaudy, cigar-puffing—
　　and women whose bodies turn garbage cans—
and then ogled my serendipitous siren,
　　once another man's wife, just as she announced,
"I've gone through a lot of men—
　　goats in togas—
and now I go through a lot of pills.
　　Loneliness is unnerving, toxic.
But most motherfuckers have elementary personalities:
　　Evil.
I've never thought that women's *Liberation* means
　　descending into muck,
but *Sex* seems to require such prosthetic stimuli
　　and lubricants—
including lurid alcohols;
　　and the *Sex* can be bravura—
with animalistic *Authenticity*,
　　so my top mouth is open, but stuffed—
and some lower-down serious bastard
　　gets me going with primal *Fuckery*—

pardon my freedom, I know,
    it's so unlady-like—
and I feel like an anxious mare
    in this horse-opera nightmare,
of rear-end coupling,
    so I begin to gag on implicit *Misogyny*,
while feeling a hearty *Mysophobia*,
    and start acting the couch-surfing adulteress,
a no-mind, nomad, no-one-man's slut,
    but next I'm curiously farting
or inhospitably, incontinently grunting,
    until strange, dark smells overwhelm.
Sex has an aesthetic of *Annihilation*.
    And what is more hateful than *Hate*?
Only *Self-Pity*."
    I studied my interlocutor.
I saw that her cosmetic was her speech—
    or her silver tongue in her onyx face;
her bitchy intelligence almost held hostage
    my lust for her glimmering thighs.
Her dress—golden—looked sunlight;
    her nipples looked piqued, thrusting
straight through her bra;
    but her mouth, her speech,
was a broken-open wound.
    To lay up in bed with her, thought I,
would be to enter a snarling, then snoring trap.

I'd ride bareback, bucking, in her cathedral,
but she'd prefer doing it while she sports
    long, white gloves, playing a Vogue *debutante?*
Yes, she's une bourgeoise with tits that quiver,
    but check the pupils of her eyes:
Are they as unscrupulous as they are unmatched?

v.

    Blinding psychedelia had detoured me
to the Pilot Tavern and this table;
    I had no economic deterrent;
I'd fooped many capable and talented
    Caucasian intellectu-elles,
scintillating, but not at *Sin*
    (if such was *Sex*),
and flaunting their lavish *schadenfreude*
    at the troubles of Nixon
and then their Freudian troubles in bed.
    They'd kicked over pedestals of *Marriage*
and *Motherhood*,
    only to mount pedestals of *Indecision*.
I now regarded madame with unbelievably blood-shot eyes
    that flickered over her peek-a-boo breasts,
her aviary-bright *avoirdupois*,
    while inhaling her intractable perfume.
So, I craved to be her silk saviour,
    to pry her saggy or stretchable snatch
until she was haggard.
    She filled my eyeballs' dimensions,
and I hoped she'd be plumb-delighted
    by my plum-tinted and plum-textured "agent,"
for she was just as stiffening of my member
    as is—well, so I've heard—*Strangulation*.
I now sprung for unbroken drinking,
    the dim honey of feral ales,
plus expensive quantities of honey-honest sherry,
    to pray for the sight of her cantering rump
after sharing French kisses as if Siamese twins,
    and doubling up in a lascivious double-bed,

so that I, a bull-like man
    could ram that lamb-tight dame,
and spring forth my constipated seed
    in a lover very, very pretty,
but pretty much coming apart at the seams,
    due to the diddling of bad men—
such as that stifling husband,
    that trifling spouse,
as despicable and as disgusting
    as shit that leeches to a shoe.

    VI.

Now came back my sabbatical down the U.S. South—
    a black tango of nooses and necks—
a space of hovel dwellers dispossessed of dreams—
    of so-called Negroes sustained
by red-clay and collard-green cheapness,
    among ravages of weeds, beetles,
ploughs gone to dust and rust
    in a landscape of vultures,
human-chewed soil, haphazard imprisonment
    (or chain-gang "employment"),
honky-tonk fascists, a conspiracy of piggy cops
    and pork-chop-fatted politicos;
a site where any hapless black
    had to squat in a cell
before returning to unyielding *Poverty*,
    all their *Ambition* ruptured,
or their balls—literally—cut off,
    or their brains shot out or heads bashed in.
But here was this luscious, chocolate Dixie *bonbon*,
    up in T.O. from da South,

who was no milky, insipid Desdemona—
    no weatherbeaten, blue-rinse *bourgeoise*—
even if she was a brow-beaten ex-mate,
    but right there under the overhead blackness
of the velvet ceiling (designed for black light),
    and present like a Christmas present,
with all of her buxom build,
    whose foundation seemed pharmaceutical,
so that now I conceived the bestial presumption
    to fuck on all-fours,
to treat the "Afro-American"
    (the newfangled slang)
to such stout engineering
    her spinal cord would sing like a violin,
and she'd get high on my sap—
    my milky, silken germs—
perhaps while still being garbed
    in her golden, upper-crust costume,
with alcohol gurgling blackly in our bellies.

VII.

Now, to leap, nude upon *Nudity*,
in infinite *Sinfulness*,
    after a lovelifetime
of numerous lies, plentiful *Valentines*,
    not because I long for *Crime*,
but because I'm committed to my *Liberty*—
    as mercilessly as is a merchant;
to dissect the spectrum
    of black-brown-beige-*blanche* belles,
to cast even brilliant bluestockings
    in wholesalely dirty, homemade blue movies.

CODA

Here's the fluorescent, if not italicized, subtext
    of "When He Was Free and Young
and He Used to Wear Silks,"
    a story as cunning as *Pessimism*,
if fundamentally realistic
    regarding politics and guessed-at (black) male attitudes
vis-à-vis masculinity and (hetero-) sexuality.
    If narration is always *Confession*,
know that *Evil* is the erection of *Nature*
    over *Reason*.

Pushkin

Sallow, callow, and proud, Pushkin*
Sashays through greening pasture.
Decades—to me—he's had no kin:
His leaves leave others manure.

His throne's a seat of cast-down pine
Laurels, posh about a tree—
Pantheon where he can recline,
Yet overshadow Shelley.

---

* *Pace* Anna Akhmatova's 1911 Russian poem (as translated and published by Vladimir Azarov and Barry Callaghan in 2013, but re-imagined by yours truly).

Hearing Peter Stein

Let everyone—the blues people—
croon their arias,

ignoring the garrote of grammar—
the corset in the throat.

Empty, empty, empty, empty, empty,
is unstrained *Harmony*.

But the Anglo-Saxons and the Americans
can be generous singers.

The only limit in *Art* is respect
for geniuses, if also jerks:

No matter how high I lift my leg,
I can't piss with the big dogs.

Yes, *Transgression* is a joy:
How can I shit the same shit as others?

One might want Hollywood—
A nude chorus or a black cow with white tits—

"Homosexual milk"—
sugar for the most base instincts—

piss for art—
assholes on T.V.:

Everything is ridiculous—Dr. Seuss or Dr. Frankenstein:
"The Fun Society" poses a "War on Terror"?!!

You must laugh about it!
A phenomenon of rubbish.

46 Cf. The monstrous—monotonous—*Excellence*
of Chekhov!

Even the Russians despair to come close to *Grandeur*
though strangely, always, they hunger:

Such brutal *Beauty* for opera fanatics....
Sold Out!

Reading Pierre DesRuisseaux

Though a poet of the precise breath,
the needling eye,
epigram & "le mot juste,"

the stringent words
slipped through teeth and lips,
teased off the tongue,

and vented from
irrefutably purifying lungs,
Pierre DesRuisseaux

delivers surprising light—
oceanic brilliance,
illuminations inextricably interwoven

like sunlit wave
splashing upon
sparkling wave—

so much light, plain light,
that he is strictly blind
to status and states,

and so erases
horizons and bias,
borders and castes....

He knows that
to be naked
is to be.

He seeks out passwords
for Heaven,
and so his poems flow

beneath the sky
like streams about stones,
incessant,

for the blood of *Liberty*
is ink,
and you'll never find leaves

more urgent than his.
His lines move sleek
as serpents,

and as voracious
as an *ado*,
wanting to treat and taste

the *Truth*.
Thus, though flesh is
irreducibly fragile,

and pages suffer erosion,
his words stay with us
as pealing waves,

the tidings of light—
the dawn sea as an extra gold mine,
or a lighthouse set eternally ablaze.

GOLD STAR

In the gloom, the gold gathers the light against it.
EZRA POUND, CANTO VII

The Light Gets In
AUSCHWITZ, MAY 2015

"How Europe Underdeveloped Africa"*

à la manière de Mao Zedong

They scrutinized Africa and espied
a Camelot of diamonds and muscle.

Toting gunpowder and cannon
and trinkets of Bibles,
the dregs of gutters and brothels,
a poxy class belching ale,
sailed—sallied—forth
to loot, shoot,
uproot, and pollute
the "Dark Continent."

They "ethereal," we "leathery":
We became the black-as-dirt shadow
to their eye-gouging, solar majesty.

They gilded themselves as gods,
branded us—literally—as barbarians,
to seize our silver and sell us on Shakespeare.

The cream of Africa
got flushed into the foaming crematoria of the Atlantic;
Worms—*et Compagnie*—
gorged on slaves, living and dead.

With *XXX* exhilaration,
the whites aped "playful" papists,
but *Rape* is a martial art,
and the issue—European, Christian—

---
* *Pace* Walter Rodney.

got baptized "niggers"
and "black bitches."

52 Cancel all bullshit blandishments:
History is Europe playing "blackface."

So is Africa now only palm wine
dripping from a brimming palm,
powerless to punch?

Forgive these boomerang dialectics,
the rhetorical questions of an unbalanced *History*,
torn between what's dead and what's new.

Africa is *Struggle* and *Spells*,
rudiments and superlatives,

and the *Negro* is circle and triangle,
and never a box,
but fluidly linear,
especially when curving
about an obstacle,
to escape,

or to go on,

resistless....

Letter from Zanzibar

After the medallion of sundown,
the gold of Zanzibar
is cloves,

but cardamom is better than silver.

 *

"A meal without wine
is breakfast;
a meal without rum
is tea."

 *

Holding chickens,
a fisherman
shows up,

then pushes off in a red mahogany *dhou*,
to gross tuna, octopus, lobster,
snapper, oysters.

The oily sea, slanting,
looks coconut
dark-brown—
only superficially white,

as dawn opens.

A black crab scuttles inside a moored *dhou*.

 *

At Stone Town,
au marché aux poissons,
spy cats, cats, cats:

Rats lurk in woodwork;
are caught dead in shadows.

    *

Charcoal-black sand plays witness
as, aloft, black crows
caw above red *dhous*,

then dive down

and scoop fish
right out the water,

teaching the charcoal-blackened fishermen
where to cast down their nets....

(In Halifax, "Africadia,"
decades back,

where black men fought white gulls
for scraps of offal at Africville's dump,

rats thought nothing
of lounging in sunlight.

Here, one sees fish-eating crows—
sophisticated carnivores—
tearing out entrails,
daintily.)

    *

At St. George Anglican Church,
in The Old English Cemetery,
overrun by skyscraping grass,

the almost-vanquished gravestones
name singular Shakespeare
and unique Thackeray:

drowned in a *Tempest* once,
their *Vanity* founders now.

Spying Mitic's (Bulletproof) "Kennedy"

à la manière de Malcolm X

The head wound is now a halo—
a special effect of the successful bullets
that gave the glamour-puss Prez
as good as he got,
shooting his 'jism'
into pricy, secretly serviced pussy....*

Thanks to Viktor Mitic's punctuation,
his definition of the photogenic visage,
those teeth that sucked Mafia cigars
and Marilyn's humongous, natural tits,
gleam ever more ferociously:

Here's the face that launched a thousand
ultimata at Castro
and kvetched at Krushchev,
but laughed off the bubble-top for the limo
when exiting Love Field:
Someone figured he was just too gold-plated
to eat lead.

Still, Mitic's ballet of holes proves J.F.K.
holier than platinum,
a deity as worthy of Warhol
as was Jackie,
this consort of babe-magnets
and vermeil magnates:
The closed-casket stud,

---

* In "Camelot,"
  He came a lot.

decorated by a state-approved arsenal,
attracts our fresh study.

Unflagging, America lines up its shots,
letting the Commander-in-Chief
give head
to his fans—
his top-guns—
and swallow incoming
like a pro,
or catch
what's up-and-coming
like a most charitable snatch.

Mitic's inimitable portrait
captures Kennedy in the bullet
"Hail
[for] the Chief,"
anthemic of—and endemic to—the U.S. Presidency.
His art goes 'Pop-Pop-Pop-Pow'
like one of Lichtenstein's day-glo tail-gunners,
lighting up critics
(or smokin dem 'assholes').

But *Terror*'s no good
unless it's "terrible
beauty,"
à la Yeats,
and that's what Mitic's "*Kennedy*" shows off—
multiple stars
(scars)
as brilliant as neon,

puncturing a mythical *Infallibility*,
yet silhouetting an icon impervious
to either bullet-spray or blood-spatter
because he already markets *Art*.

Is this portrait an action painting
of a White House James Bond,
so bullets spurt and blood flies,
and the subject is put down,
canvassed,
like graffiti art,
knocked off quick and dirty,

or like the Black Dahlia's Cubist corpse?

Who can say? *If* it's disreputable,
it's no more cheap
than Hollywood *Virtue*
(tinsel)
or Washington *Truth*
(confetti).

Anyway, Mitic makes us see again,
through his reverse Braille,
how frail all our saints are,

perforated
by the very cinematic light
they project.

Black Power!
LISBON, MARCH 2009

A Draft Elegy for B.A. (Rocky) Jones

*à la manière d'*Yevgeny Yevtushenko

I.

I don't want to write this elegy—
not for Rocky—
not for Burnley Allan Jones—
because no coffin can frame him,
no words can take his measure;
he doth orbit beyond obituaries....

But he was unprecedented *Excellence*,
outta all Nova Scotia:
He lit up even daylight like a flare
because he had game, had flair,
like a copper black flame—
irrefutably black—
the brilliant epitome of never diminished blackness.....

Spy him spookin the T.V.:
Shaft gone intellectual.

The very air got impregnated with his black leather—
never scruffy—
but indelible, chic—
suitable to a scientist of speech
as bright and biting as a knife—
heroic chrome,
dazzling, sure, but no mere accessory.

Check:
When Rocky had to stand up for *Justice*—

or had to stand up for us—
Black (*et*) Mi'kmaq—
Africadian—
he showed the poise
and took the pose
of a hammer quick to strike.

Don't deem his bravado merely pantherish!
His stride was lightning tearing cross our eyes,
and his rappin struck us upside the head
with thunderous shocks:

Dude unleashed zingers and zest—
sound bites with teeth—
and handsome laughter—
vivid, ferocious.

The chap was earthy
and down-to-earth,
plain-spoken because
lying is an abuse of *Time*.

Rocky's talk shot straight stereo to our ears.
He demanded that we demand
that *Law* act *Righteous* by us.

He couldn't bring any routine medicine:
He saw that he had to fumigate
every sanctimonious cranny
of every legislature and every church.

Job 1 for him?
Discombobulate the Oppressor!

He took home the Order of Nova Scotia
for trying to end the disorder of Nova Scotia—
all the discord and disaster of Bluenose racism.

So Rocky stood his ground—
on sand or flinty soil.
Never a bystander,
he helped us to "overstand"—
right outstandingly.

Helplessly joyous in his hope for us,
he preached that *Hope* is a catalyst:
(For the hopeless, *can-do*'s got *done-in*.)

Rocky brought no fleeting gifts—
he was solid-state,
down with the People.
He was the true do-gooder,
rowdy, with steady nerves.

Admit that he was scintillating—
and terrifyingly tall.
Casual in his languid nobility,
but ready to produce *Wit*
and induce *Delight*,
Rocky would step into a room,
and all the gravity therein
would prove specific to him.

He was like inimitable poetry,
perfect in any translation.

Never any atrocious, politic rhetoric,
his talk leafed through intangible but priceless volumes.

Nor would he hobnob with snobs—
the guys with button-down degrees
and pointless appointments.
Rocky liked folks to prove as factual—
as sweet-and-sour, Chinese takeout.

Comin to us live from Truro,
proud outta Truro,
he was never confused—
and not one bit foolish.
Rocky knew the bite of *Keith's** ale
and the kick of a rifle,
and the dip of a fishing line.

We can name the sell-outs:
They don't *represent*;
they *front*.
Those are dollar signs that were their eyes.
These bourgeois coddle *Injustice*,
relax, collect brand-name luxuries—
Gucci this, *Versace* that.
They claim that they're "on fire,"
but all they are is piss with a temperature.
No one can place Rocky in such company.
He never dealt with any stuck-up culture—
no Parliament Hill or Beverley Hills airs.
He couldn't fit in
with the 'in' crowd.
He was too good an outsider,
because he cometh out the Marsh.

I began this poor elegy apologizing,
dreading this writing.

---

* Correct pronunciation: *Keats*.

I still do.
But *Poetry* revives the cemetery'd,
and survives the cemetery....

    ii.

As I write, I see the man himself.
Rocky could rock a top hat
while rockin a canoe;
I spy the "subversive" out there,
anglin a line and hook
through a river's dangerous chuckles.
Later, he drowns a cold beer in his belly,
then fires up a trout,
enjoying ale and fish
in the intrepid cold of dusk,
a fitting finish
to a day of thought and talk and laughter—
the dividing line of his face.

Rocky could whistle up
a salt moon, a sugar moon,
a moon as weightless as milkweed fluff,
and he knew how trout look up
at shaken up stars.

(He heard *Nature* as *Spiritual* because—
To listen,
One must be silent.)

Misfortune's medals are tears.
Our eyes have minted them
and must mint them still.

But Rocky would have us spend
our silver tears and diamond sweat

in the struggle

to make money worthless—

compared with breath.

In Homage to Garry Thomas Morse

The attempt to impose "Empire"—
to police *Nature* through the prism of a grid—
rectangles, squares, parallels—
betrays what isn't possible,
but constructs such cages
that showcase *Anthropology*
as a case of *Zoology*;

as if the effort to interdict the organic
is, *pace* Atwood,
a "progressive insanity"
of the settler too unsettled
in his/her *dis/location*—
uprooting and transplant—
to know the new landscape
as its own civilization;
not "wilderness" *per se*,
but a government of wind
and lightning,
grasslands and Lake-de-la-Woods.

Garry Thomas Morse interrogates
this dilemma in his verse-outlay,
his odyssey-outlier,
Prairie Harbour
(Talonbooks, 2015),
wherein one finds the full flowering
of ideas sprouted in Robert Kroetsch's *Seed Catalogue*,
for the First Nations bard riffs on Shakespeare—
as if that 400-year-old ghost
is shakin his spear

at interlopers onto the Prairies
who don't imagine Head-Smashed-In-At-Buffalo-Jump
as bred-in-the-bone brain surgery—
as a culling—harvest—of dreams.

Survey Morse's *Prairie Harbour*
as if the author's Eli Mandel,
brandishing Greco-Latin codes,
spiking *Indian Act* misinterpretations,
Gothic as barbed-wire.

Read closely and you will recall horses
pitching in stables,
as a blaze tramples darkness pell-mell,
and the inferno unfurls—
stretches impetuous into gallop—
leaping cubicle upon cubicle—
while each horse mane bristles and flares
with a profane crimson,
and equine bodies—
already in persistent undress—
race from tan or umber
or copper or white
to a stripped-down, denuded charcoal—
searing, signal blackness—
the skeletal, airy grime of smoke,
itself tumbling after the prancing flames,
the promenading flames,
the insolent illumination of a *Sovereignty*
that's kin to Prairie fire—
destructive, but clarifying.

But Morse inks no epitaph of *Sorrow*
in *Prairie Harbour*.
His Apollonian stallions and mares
are not nightmares of burnt bones,
tatters of teeth,
but wild, untameable horses—
as free as fire—
as liberated as smoke—
exactly what the prehistoric
Wakashan Constitution proposes:
That we walk in harmony with the wind.

*Principles of Good Governance**

In Memory of Two Eminent Torontonians:
Dr. Sheela Basrur, O.Ont (1956–2008)
& Mr. Charles Roach, LL.B (1933–2012)

I. BACKGROUND PAPER

1. Educate the electorate.

2. *Illiteracy* rots *Democracy*.

3. Equality? Fine schools, fine teachers, in *every* district.

4. The *Citadel of Reason*? The *Library*.

5. Quote *Scripture*; cite *History*; recite *Poetry*.

6. Do not plague the people by shouting drivel.
   Do not demonize opponents.
   Do not mislead or confuse.
   Produce *Facts*.

7. *Honesty* is State *Treasure*.

8. A governor's speech must be as clear as water.

9. *Clarity* is a branch of *Charity*.

10. To be decisive,
    First be incisive.

---

* The poem riffs on Confucius (via Pound), Machiavelli, Sun Tzu, several Tang Dynasty and Song Dynasty poets.

11. *Judgment* must be as cool as steel, as sharp as steel.

12. To convince is better than to conquer.

13. *Complaint* is *Revelation*.

14. *News* perpetually startles,
    Yet its truths are ancient:
    To the *Perceptive*.

15. Do not pander; also, do not puff up superiors.

16. *Flattery* is bribery; it is slush.

17. *Excuses* enshrine *Cowardice*.

18. Remember: Great *Thought* leaps upward—
    To try to discern *Divinity*.

II. ON LAWMAKING

1. Political success? A silver tongue and a heart of gold.

2. Elected? Serve the people.

3. *Sobriety*, *Punctiliousness*, *Generosity*, and *Intelligence*:
   These qualities demand allegiance.

4. *Ethics* is a scythe,
   Separating the correct from the corrupt.

5. Even the bad governor envies good policies.

6. The heedless governor is soon headless.

7. Good laws set themselves good examples.

8. *Extremism* only serves thermometers.

9. *Excess* disguises *Dysfunction*.

10. *Egoism* is *Insufficiency*.

11. *Envy* dreams up conspiracies.

12. Err in one law?
    Correct it in the next.

13. The law suit never fits—
    Unless it's a straitjacket.

14. First, comprehend *Justice*;
    Then, apprehend criminals.

15. Dust dwells and swells—
    When the broom is stayed.

16. Police secrecy equals *Sedition*.

17. Citizens must be governors;
    Lest they be oppressed.

18. Plant vineyards, not prisons.
    Plant vineyards; cart home the city wine.

III. ON ECONOMY

1. The *Treasury* is for the citizens' convenience.

2. Sacrosanct is *Renminbi**.

3. *Capital* flows;
   Labour pools.

4. Greatness? Public works, public art.

5. Spend: Do not let potholes become sinkholes.

6. *Beauty* demands *Maintenance*.

7. When in *Debt*, build.
   When in *Doubt*, build.
   Paper *Wealth* is air:
   Build.

8. *Diversity* rouses *Beauty*.
   (*Light* does not discriminate.)

9. Nurture
   Infrastructure,
   Agriculture,
   Manufacture,
   Architecture,
   Arts & Culture—
   To richly prosper.

10. Create, profit; save, invest;
    Create, profit; save, invest.

---

* Chinese: The people's money; i.e., yours and mine.

11. To secure heaven, help the lowly.

12. *Benevolence* staves off *Violence*.

13. *Charity* engineers *Miracles*.

14. *Plutocracy* vomits black bread, black flags, and black batons.

15. *Arms* dig *Deficits*.

16. *Spending* should be like planting,
    Never like eating.

17. *Taxation* should be transfusion,
    Not vampirism.

18. Squander revenues, spark revolts.

19. *Paltry* is that government careless of *Poetry*.

IV. ON BEAUTY

1. *Youth* creates; *Age* preserves.

2. Revere children; respect elders.

3. Sun is balm; rain is ointment.

4. *Light* allows no doubt.

5. Good *Style* wins popularity;
   Good *Deeds* inspire devotion.

6. Be a Caesar to allies and a Sphinx to adversaries.

7. *Beauty* escapes *Chastisement*.

8. Good wine precedes good *Poetry*.
   Good wine succeeds good *Poetry*.

GOLD HEART

*He bent me back..., tore my legs from around him
and shoved them up; gold was exposed to him....*
A.X. HOLMSBY, *BLACK IS BEAUTIFUL (BUT IS IT A NO-NO?)*

Gold is worth but gold;/ Love's worth love.
ALGERNON CHARLES SWINBURNE, "CHILD'S SONG"

The Kiss (of Death)
VENICE, APRIL 2010

Venus: An Anatomy

Her catastrophic nudity
Fells male, female, in fouling *Vice*.
Our agile, gleaming enemy,
Some Dante-designed, dream-debris,
Is born in flames, but damned to ice.
Her catastrophic nudity
Displays dingy and dour ivory—
White quite vile and viral—like lice.
Our agile, gleaming enemy—
Half Sappho, but half Salomé—
Takes *Lust*'s camphor, sulphur, for spice.
Her catastrophic nudity,
Her ogress sex, her tigress glee—
Destroy but once, betray but twice.
Our agile, gleaming enemy—
Medusa-styled, "drag" Kabuki—
Racks us with '*Love*' like Anti-Christ's.
Her catastrophic nudity
Shows agile, gleaming *Enmity*.

On Reading 'Teacher's Pets' by Crystal Hurdle

A classroom seducer triumphs by the score:
His old, bold, gold-haired, sweaty thighs
Imp surprising dew on needle-tight eyes,
While fresh-wilted waists waft *calore* galore,

Plus unimaginable, quite indelible *Guilt*
(At teach's spunky *Gratification*),
Then feelings congealed once tears have spilt—
The body wavering twixt *Exhilaration*

(The recall of succulent caresses,
The tempest of sweat), but also the recoil
From the man's repellent successes
With other girls, his greedy *Lust* to despoil.

But doesn't *Hedonism* almost always mean
He-done-me, *he-done-her*, and so *he-done-wrong*,
Til obvious torments now turn obscene
And what seemed *Love* proves *Lust* all along?

Hurdle's verses suggest *Love* is *mascavado*—
Impure—that taproom tears bathe bedroom eyes;
That *Love* is semi-*maso*, pseudo-*sado*,
That *Law* upholds faulty, weak-flesh philosophies.

A courtroom puts a bedroom in a brutal light.
Is "he-said, she-said" always black-and-white?
Or more like shifty grades of grey—
When pillow talk echoes lip-synch play?

"La philosophie dans le boudoir"

à la manière de Sade

    When Herr Heidegger caught Fraulein Arendt,
Philosophy fit taut—or meet, nixing
Fixed *Sin*. In her sweet course, his discourse tapped
Honeyed *Feeling*, nourishing *Thought*, divorced
From Nazi dogma—acid—or Nietzsche's
Vinaigrette palette. She sweated him free—
The professor—until he could savour
Bare *Truth*: Any *Philosophy* cleavered
From *Flesh*, from *Hunger* and *Satisfaction*,
Issues tart, acidic *Hypocrisy*.
    But he was like a man who, once seeing clear
His mirrored face, forgets the sight, and so,
Having studded his student, turned,
Returned to tears—as a dog does vomit.

"Mariangela E La Seduzione"

*à la manière d'*Ennio Morricone

Not a woman to put by, to keep for
Breaking, entering, Mariangela*
Embodies *Melting*, what heats an outcast
Intruder, ice-eyed, who can't love, but fucks.

A Canuck snowdrop, with a poppy heart,
Her silky pot prompting minute murmurs,
Then attic moans, she's fragrance he leafs through,
Once they're as joint as four walls plus corners.

Now, "Christ," shouted, chimes hotly in the tryst,
Overturning the palace of her skirt;
And the fine-ass, small-tit wench shakes as if
Martha Beck, quaking her electric chair.

Up at dark, her eyelash winks at bony
Starlight, as, unquiet, his flesh starts fresh riot.

―――――――
Cf. Laura Antonelli.

"Desolazione Cosmica"

*à la manière d'*Angelo Lavagnino

Unsheathe your slick, orgulous instrument,
Pickle it in that snacking gash; sink black
Twixt its two coral halves—like a raven
Chipping at a dripping watermelon.

Enterprise, dip, slurp, raging, feverish—
As if you'll never again taste such fruit,
Fleshy, drooling, until your eyes dirty
With tears, and elongated *Arrogance*

Withers, a-wallow in *Oblivion*.
(*Nature* is vigorous in withering.)
You ravish it; she kills you completely.
Yes, you rise again, raven, out her cave,

But, ravenous, return to trap—and meal....
You perform; you eat; are eaten, deformed.

"Lei Se Ne Muore"

*à la manière d'*Ennio Morricone

Velvety clamps—her hands—lock down my thighs.
Pressure—unpleasantly pleasurable—
Squeezes me to squalid *Release*.
A roused tigress, she aggresses, greedy.

I snapped, "If you're hungry, try some of this!"
With flair, she—her total sex—snatched at it.
(*What a feeling! Excitement!*) Inside her—
A blinding dampness, a splendid swamp,
Indigestible snot, a snake canal—
Ooze I slurp, and bile I can really taste.

Pig-sloppy, grunting, and trotting in sheets,
We muster musty stench of mud and musk.

Ecstatic cawing completes our rutting—
Our feeding without eating: Twin Zombies.

"Rapimento Grottesco"

*à la manière d'*Ennio Morricone

Anorexic, athletic, the lithe slut
Makes *Anatomy* our *Gastronomy*:
Gluttonous slobbering leaves me gasping
Her salmon Eden—thanks to her grasping mouth.

Tilting at her guiltless, coltish juncture,
The puckered jewel sliding succulently,
I'm put down like a fat aristocrat
Giving head to a guillotine. *Bravo!*

A piano stroked by an axe, I groan.
Glistens her flooded sex—fiery, sopping,
Felicitous. She grins. My scowl's dashing—
A fleet robber crashing a flashlight's beam.

Bottles totter; wine sinks fangs in two throats.
Mon dieu! But it's a mauve, delicious wine!

"Drammi Gotici"

*à la manière d'*Ennio Morricone

After their fuming *Industry*, she smokes.
He scuttles to her sink to scour off her smell.
His soiled face sours in her toilet's mirror:
Her superb perfume spoils. *What just happened?*

They had guffawed like two well-pleased butchers.
Her hindering garments dissolved, shredded—
Like sunlight-disintegrated moonlight:
His phallus spelunked pell-mell in the gal.

At their peak, the inimical *Pinnacle*,
They'd composed twin, sweaty, shiny demons—
Ivory *Matrix* and ebony *Totem*.
Their alliance—its salience—was one of *Loss*.

Now erect, pathetic in her bathroom,
He's skeletal Golliwog, collapsing.

Guess who's afraid of V. Woolf!
MALTA, AUGUST 2011

Oreo Blues

Darkness thuds down with rain:
Night's jellied mud oozes a swamp!
Darkness giggles with rain:
Feel blackness jump and stomp!
My big-ass gal's white in vain,
Muck besmirches all her pomp.

A piebald suburb welcomes
Mescal-white worm, black-earth sex.
Smut befuddles Negroid slums,
Tormenting *Happiness*. Hex
Hypocrites in Christian homes:
Orgasms gleam—ivory, onyx.

A dyed-in-the-wool Negro,
I'm a hung man when we kiss.
She's Dixie; I'm an "oreo":
Each is traitor to each race.
If we're caught out, see me go—
Spectacles, Swiss watch, suitcase.

I feel lonesome as a flower,
Glorious in a desert!
Like a *Qur'an* in a liquor store,
I'm misplaced; I'm dissed; I'm hurt.
My gal sucked all my gusto;
I'm like Autumn-cut-down August: Curt.

We're as public as children—
Giving vent to our juices,
Wet as the black, raining din,
Blue as Louisiana bruises:
Love is a listing beacon—
A fire fainting in sluices.

We're cheek-by-jowl to *Doom*,
A black/white *Porgy and Bess*.
Lovemaking in torrid gloom—
Sordid where *Love* protests.
Best I scram from this room—
Or I die a dissected mess.

Abandonment

à la manière de Saint-John Perse

I sought her whom my soul loveth.
I was languishing, drooling like a dog.

I brought no painted bottle of Chianti.
I brought a dark, crimson wine, subtle as smoke.

I wanted our bed to turn a cake,
with frosting spilled about.

But that woman,
Nature's own tart,
that wine-guzzling wench,
as white as froth,
and her hair all gold and her body all gorgeous,
whose fine mouth sweats only *Sweetness*—
that Nova Scotianess—
who sings hymns in church
but squeals like a whore in bed
(or squeals like a bride under her bridegroom)—
I can't embrace or fondle,
I don't fondle and embrace,
for she won't be wooed to wed.
(Brass jingles when she shakes the bed.)

Now, both rusty dusk and blood-red dawn,
I bear leaden sorrow as heavy as iron.
She won't be mine, no, not unless her church okays a brothel!
(She's a bad woman; will make a bad wife, a bad mother.)

Call me a dandy harlequin, a handy fool.

I'll tramp into New Brunswick;
I'll hike out of Nova Scotia—
dark Nova and dreary Scotia—
the sea's stronghold—
where the Atlantic swamps sailors
and scuppers their ships.

I'll forget the sumptuous sea chanteys of Nova Scotia....

Nothing here ain't wind-molested.
No trivial breeze rebuffs me.
This air has fangs.
(You see the sea?
Its brine is my undrunk wine.)

The wind bawls denunciations.
Trees shriek back.

I must cross over to New Brunswick—
that province topped with stars—
to find a better, unbitter woman—
a dirty, little pigeon,
merry with her salacious favours—

likely down in Saint John,

down on 47 Moore Street,*

down on all fours....

Cf. George Hamilton, *circa* January 8, 1949.

"Malinconica Serenità"

*à la manière d'*Ennio Morricone

Unblemished wine!
Wine showing a lion's growling spirit!
Some contumacious *Nectar*, reminiscent

Of an elegant, dusky gal, smelling of lilies—
A black-silk Creole splurging on *parfum*—
I mean, smoky with aroma—

Majestic to relish (like licorice),
To ravish and shiver honey within—
Sounding her slippery, alert, and dexterous maw.

Floods of gold-plated wine!
Niagaras of lily-scented *eau-de-toilette*!
Kisses pooling, then swamping lips!

Untarnished blackness, slutty girlish *Lust*,
Then oiled ebony poling a citrus cleft.

"Amore In Fiore"

à la manière de Piero Piccioni

Field volcanic, unladylike fucking—
Summery *Misery*—as you groan, moan,
And buck—squealing and squawking like a gull:
Each virgin's thus fixed for crucifixion.

But you crave pinning, not pin-up poems, eh?
Swell! I come—barbarian to my bowels—
To plunger your pivotal cavity,
Rosy limbo, and there, like black smoke, swivel.

Our satires on *Depravity* lather
And plaster you with froth, venomous streaks.
But you mince, wince, and mewl agreeably,
Are liberally dirtied, but yell, *"Oui! Oui!"*

We chafe and chafe until we foam *Champagne*,
Then break like mirrors—our selves' splintered panes.

Editoriale

Fuck, sweet ladies! Fuck all you want!
Fuck so you jostle the deceased.

Imitate oceans: Go naked—
And be as seething and swamping.

Love voraciously! Swallow up,
Then spit out, each kinky cynic.

Horses churn up foam, so should you:
So fuck until you crash and burst.

Never recant! Don't cant: Canter!
Angels, give all and take all.

Whether clean, dirty, or washed up,
Your anatomy needs stuffing.

So, fuck, ladies! Fuck all you want!
Fuck so you jostle the deceased!

GOLD LEAF

Nature's first green is gold....
ROBERT FROST, "NOTHING GOLD CAN STAY"

January Trees, or A Civil Elegy

For Dennis Lee, Poet Laureate of Toronto, 2000–04

Winter *rigor mortis*: This clockwork lock-down.

The City has already carted off
ugly, disintegrating Xmas trees,
sprawled like ex-dictators' staggered statues
or delirium tremens drunks,
occupying disinterested sidewalks;

it's also trucked away the black remains
of sloughed-off leaves,
lest they clog the sewers.

(No *Civilization* without working sewers.)

One clear advantage of truculent winter is,
we recognize our severely inferior infrastructure—
lampposts, cellular towers, satellite dishes,
skyline-disfiguring erections—
not as incremental blight,
or as a retinal pox,
but as casual, copasetic trophies.

Without their fledgling garments—
that leap and spring of green,
we can view the now-thin trees—
maples standing as squirrel-scoured skeletons,
as so much municipal puffery—
real-estate street-views suited for price-fixing
high-income neighbourhoods.

Otherwise, a tree is disreputable urbanity, eh?
Each one seems to upbraid us
for ignoring the sun, or the breeze,
as we shunt or scrunch through glass canyons
or zigzag through cops-and-stoners alleys,
or skid down brand-new asphalt,
almost avoiding pedestrian impediments.

(No wonder eyesore architects omit trees,
classify them as spindly monsters,
sneaky as weeds,
spurting up from grass,
or practising a civic vampirism,
biting into lawns,
rooting into pipes,
uprooting concrete,
and turning *For-Sale* lots
into dangerously entrancing, Transylvanian forest.)

Now, January snow is a collapsed firmament,
lending the darkest towers a murky gleam,
but sprucing up every derelict thing,
its fluorescent spread
creaming trees too.

Despite frigidity,
pining for such light,
we venture out,
ogle the pared-down trees,
spy the now-bared, sunlight-sweet nests
that await fresh flicker—
wings peeling from air,

and maybe we ourselves recall
the autumnal *Joy* of stripping naked,

how every blooming tree is an *effeuilleuse*
once per calendar,

that *Nudity* is
looking up at God,

and our own velvet sinews realize
the unveiled revelation of *Elation*—

how *Nature* holds tenure.

Nature holds tenure....

Yep: the January maple
(let's say)
looks scrawny elder—
withered, wan, wind-blasted,
no more than a standing shadow—

but the truth is

that tree is pregnant.

Early Spring in the Annapolis Royal Historic Gardens

> *"All shine in the dust,*
> *All the same Novice Scotia."*
> JACK KEROUAC, "216TH-C CHORUS"

This grey, frigid, wind-flayed, March Sunday—
the "Innovative Garden" says "not yet," not "yes":
It fields closed buds and brown-black leaves
and winter cabbage that looks dowdy,
gone pale-green or dead-purple.
Shrivelled weeds and grisly fragments—
studs—
of pallid green crop up here and there—
like gangrene bone shards after a plane crash....

Snow shrouds, or strives to shroud, all:
Its cold sweat glistens,
but is too frail to touch.

Even graveyards splay snow-scoured;
frost glazes the dust
and otherwise dull, dingy grass,
each brown blade its own soft, anonymous headstone.

A path pays out slick green, brown spruce needles:
Slipping—
or irreverent, accidental, backbone-breaking "skating"—
is a winter expedient.

Over a field of see-through snow,
dog paws chase
three-pronged bird-tracks.
Crows caw a raucous, kiss-my-arse chorus.

A brisk wind prods me into the vacant rose garden,
just as fresh snow flares, snares,
annoying,
like hail:

There's been too much already!
(Banished cold, that's summer!)

Winter lingers so long,
our weariness becomes *Worry*.

December defoliates all,
and January is as injurious as *Time*.
February is as boisterous
and as vicious as untrue *Valentines*.
March ushers in the caustic whiteness
of squall and squelching slush,
so winter seems to plaster all
as irrevocably as *Gravity*.

So much *Beauty* just faints—
like political promises.

I tromp on white snow that's crusty,
beneath the superficial softness,
and view rime-wracked roses—
only thorns now, bushels of thorns,
the blooms all deadheaded.
The plants look spindly cacti—
and yet *Beauty* will burst from these stems—
intoxicating, erotic, tea-scent tantalizing—
once March ebbs to May-month charms.

Now, my pen must push through snow pellets—
striking and sticking to the wind-dickered page.

I close my book; the snow stops.
I open it again, and my fingers freeze.

Near me, there's a puddle—
impossibly solvent water!
It should be ice—
at least a silken lockup!

The pond looks a sepulchral mirror.

(Ice paints even rain white.)

Maps preserve nothing.

I glance over at the railway bridge—
its iron's rusted,
the colour of dry blood—
the sordid ink of *Geopolitics*.

The sky hulks grey-white, white-grey,
and blustery over the gold-brown marsh;
clouds seem thin, shy pearls—
as plain as unwritten poems.

My fingers feel freshly numb—
my pages turn corpse-cold—
black ink flits, drops, crow-like.

I'm a clerk,
skulking among snow,
voicing vain verses to the wind,

that bullish, bullhorn roar:

The Fundy tide be a-comin in!

The Annapolis River flings forth petals
of drops,
so many ice-sheathed tears,
arriving as all-pervasive swells.

Currents collapse, muddled, upon mudbanks.

This cold spring, late March, feels unbearable—
just damp, dark, and demoralizing;
the cold wet showering down
is just sleazy hygiene.

I open a gate unto bullrushes, cattails,
and winds hit as hard as a freight train.

I stand now where tracks once lay.

Drizzling snow hazes the Gardens
with blurs of cream.

Harsh looks the marsh and the hills beyond—
just snow and spruce and fir and pine and snow—
but the snow now blooms
as if to cancel buds.

My fingers, freezing, I gotta leave off ink.

I yield to the white chill,
the lily-bleaching snow—
the drizzling *grisaille*—
this torrent of cobwebs!

There's no pristine sunlight here.
Instead, tree branches share slices of light,
facets of shadow,
while chill still abounds.

(Is *Goodness* graspable
when cold clasps the hand?)

In pure, Nova Scotian exhaustion,
as dusk turns snow to dust-like stars,
I back off from writing up these gardens,
hardening again with dark and ice,
until April—
metaphysical April—
renews a fiscal legacy
of burnt grass and churned earth
and blossom and dandelion and milkweed
and tax returns and geese returning.

I've seen—tried to see—enough.

I exit, hoping for grog.

Look it!
A crow whickers upward in the glorious finale of light.

The poet is a voyageur:

Because nothing is as voyeuristic as light.

Reverie of The Commons

Us North End kids swarmed an emerald-bright prairie—
a free oasis more dirt than grass—
where bats whacked or bopped baseballs
and sneakers slid—or skidded—to safety
(or jerks got put out)
in shiny, obstreperous dust—
summer sunlight gone gritty.

We'd bike or hike, slog or jog,
to-and-fro The Commons,
us nat'chal-bo'n Communists,
sharing pop and chips,
or following our partisan instinct,
to egg on hysterics—fist-fights—
cheering each bloody face
with a hullabaloo like Stradivarian clarions,
and being most happy when we saw proof
that bones are as fragile as beer bottles.

Those fights were terrible squalls, pitiless,
because the combatants—
navy brats, kung-fu cadets—
wanted to prove the other worthless,
just a chump from up by The Dump,
or a "bastard" or a "retard"
or some "dummy" from the shipyard.

But all us were, to some inspecting eyes—
so much gutter "scum":
Us were *la racaille* of "Maniac" Square,
les miz of "*Götterdämmerung*" Street,
just a bunch of blue-collar and pink-collar
and black-ass *sans-culottes*.

Still we took to that cavalcade of greenery—
The Commons—
teeming,
to execute kaleidoscope-colourful collisions
of scar-face teams—
baseball, football,
and hockey
(once the Egg Pond iced).

As "pickaninnies," as no-damn-good "punks,"
monkeying about—
going ape on monkeybars,
or doing monkeyshines in the pools
or on the merry-go-round—
we could also pretend pirates
and treat the museum-piece, Grizzly tank
as an earthbound shipwreck,
or view swings as being as expectant as doors,
or dream we were defending cardboard-box forts
against a hurricane of spears
(i.e. twigs),
with The Armouries staring us down,
planning patiently for our adult dispatch
to Bosnia, Haiti, Afghanistan, etc.,
as Her Majesty's Dour-or-Dead Canucks....

The Commons was our trod-down garden,
where milkweed shudders under rain,
and gulls go gaga,
trying to snatch our *al fresco*, Vachon cakes and "samwiches"
while we strove to avoid the daily red-face drunk,
blood-shot in nose and eye,
and his bullying, wine-breath wench,

some wobbling trollop—
off Trollope Street, eh?

Under flickering lightning—
that wasting brightness—
then dirty drizzle
or the plump plop of each raindrop,
we never felt betwixt-and-between,
but did dillydally indoors
to scare up music or finger paint
or pretzel foolhardy *Play-Doh*,
and tilt trombones to burp, "Yippee!",
Trumpets bray, "Whee!",
Our rabid singing hounding wriggling, wiggling notes.

Later, under crumbled or splintered sunlight—
a beige sun, a whitewash sky—
someone would pull up cups of buttercups,
or there'd be a clash in mud
(the tossing of clumps that splattered like the napalm
splashing Vietnam/Cambodia).

The teens and elders of our neighbourhood
knew The Commons as a *lumpen* brothel,
where miracles of *Kool-Aid* and alcohol
could whisk knickers off,
and a mate could cop a feel of nookie
hitherto only imagined
in thumbing dirty books
strewn about school-grounds by trashy sailors.

Soon, some'd try out mackerel positions—
sporadic flip-flops

in spiteful dust,
or'd just do "it" in the grass,
scoring green lacerations
from those emergency, godsend beds—
the plots behind a bush,
good for a sweet, sultry, swearing jade,
who'd find her womb cradling sperm
come milky daybreak.

(Aye, in daylight, it was easy to spot
the languorous messiness
of lower-class lovers,
who'd left no blade of grass unmussed,
and whose blue jeans' pale seats
now showed verdant stains.)

The Commons was listless wildness, surely.
But the fountain drenched us like a floundering cloud,
full of insolent rain
(way better than the swimming pools—
those habitats made acrid
by blasphemous bladders and chlorine).

It was a civic baptism, of sorts,
and our halo was always
a sudden circling of gulls.

Green/Light: A Chronicle of Sun

For Dionne Brand, Poet Laureate of Toronto, 2009–12

"The Fall"—
Empyreal—

downcomes

livid in seething air—
gold leaves, lavishly, coldly blazed, dead—
plus crimson leaves, vivacious with death....

Quick, our florid redoubts
are stripped,
splintered into sticks.

Every park shows bony ruins—
a flagrant demolition.

Thus, November numbs us.
Soil, suppurating, oozes ochre juices.
Sunflowers, frost-charred, snap,
collapse,
just dull, seedy tissue.

Our gardens bristle—
horripilate under horrid winds—
turn brushy bouquets—
sprout thorns, spikes, pricks.

Civilized bush, that's Toronto,
bro!

December sleigh-rides home:
Blunt whiteness all about.

See Santa—
down-to-earth as frost,
hearty as a hearth:
He's no half-hearted honcho.

But we're sometimes as dispirited
as ice—
all that jailed water.

Our TVs flicker on.
Sharp tongues harp on and on,
sound profoundly

Idle No More—

damning Unoriginal Sins
gainst th'Original Citizens.

(*Justice* is slowpoke as a cumulus,
or as swift and exact as lightning.)

By New Year's,
there's the prowling glitter
of moonlight on solid white:

Winter parades
in a mask of snow.

Our urban forest blanches—
blizzarded by whitewash mapmakers
(imperialists)—

dissolving fences and sacking flowers
and wiping away paths and lanes—

in night's ethereal charcoal—
under moonlight's ragamuffin pewter.

Our walks are only chestnut-shadowed
after each pungent, obnoxious thaw.

Upon *Aprilis*,
we apprehend
the comprehensive *annus mirabilis*
insurgent Spring mounts.

Lo! Rain spikes down;
branches take vociferous baptism,
simultaneously,
as the disconcerting slush
pushes off,
before the seditious surfacing of grass—
so extra, extra green.

Now cometh woozy penetration
of roots, thrusting into lawns—
a weedy cabal,
balkanizing—
nursed and rehearsed greenery—
perennials, preening.

Still, rain raves and riots on:

Hear a montage
of gutters, drains, ravines,
slurping

each beautiful trickle.

Or there's the steel-pan vivacity
of wetness rattling rooves,

and rinsing mud off gold,
upping garage-sale prices.

Spy the damp amber of sun,
afterwards—

that Van Gogh sun,
a replica in beaming tobacco leaf!

Persistent is the pine scent
of pining.

Maples wriggle;
lilacs boast spirited petals.

Parks revel in plumage.

The gay spontaneity of birdsong
graces Spring's green frieze,

cheers pupils and pensioners alike.

Floréal, *Nisan*, reign:

Blossom petals snow,
cascade, kissing earth.

We don wreaths of vines,
never rue;

sip sweet dew, beneficent dew.

Come again the sunflowers—
a wind-blown blaze.

Now thunder barks,
and we find balmy calm—

th'egalitarian satisfactions
of love, delight,
shade, shelter,

refuge,

wherever the light—

greening—

bids us park.

His Pound of Flesh
VENICE, APRIL 2010

À Rapallo

Apollo-blessèd Rapallo
Is, at palm-tree shore, rococo,
Not tawdry or tourist-hollow....
Thanks to bronze-tinting sirocco,

Each polar pallor palliates,
As wine-persuaded women loll,
Displaying silky delicates—
Beauty that trumps all folderol—

Tits expertly pert, asses—bright
In threads, gossamer, milky, chic—
Lacy, frail, lucid panties, quite
Infallible on bling physique.

Precociously flint-hearted girls,
Belles as *bella* as Dante's belles,
Fritter gilt away; all unfurls
As they fall: Punic Hannibals.

This glimmering port boasts *Glamour*—
The opulence of wind, wanton,
Insolent, refreshing summer—
Forum of sexy exhibition.

As raucous as seagulls, tourists
Flock to snap each well-lapped vista:
Crappy whores, unceremonious,
They disdain the command, "*Basta!*"

Villa Riviera applauds
Hemingway, who stayed—drunk—and wrote.
Omit "the eyesore of his words":
His fame is all they care about.

Along each lustrous labyrinth,
View tiles scintillant as the sea.
Tread like Pound feigning bafflement—
Incorrigibly jittery.

This hub of wind, this yacht-club-stage
Of *Love*, is blue and blinding haze
Ferrying a whiff of Carthage
History's dumb voyeurs erase.

Unlikely likeable, this town—
Refuge that Yeats blazoned "Chinese"—
A quarantine that crowns *Renown*—
Dissatisfies all elegies.

GOLD COAST

*One [Toronto skyscraper] facing him, built
almost entirely out of glass, shimmers like gold.*
AUSTIN C. CLARKE, "CANADIAN EXPERIENCE"

T-or-*ont*-au

MALTA, AUGUST 2011

Bridge Crossing

I.

The locomotive forwards steel, aluminum;

it thrusts from a womb of *Bliss*—
shows that hurtling health that's *Speed*—

asserts a right-of-way—
i.e., the right to be
free—

not "Underground," but "above-ground,"
an up-and-coming—
overcoming—
railway,

that delivers one and all to offices,
factories, homes,
overturning every mooring.

The railway train tornadoes
through cloaks-and-daggers—
vigilantes in white robes brandishing dark guns—
the lynchers-in-rags—
the fractured ingenuity of *Apartheid*,
home-grown—

and/or verminous cops—

and pushes aside
the flat, grey-faced mobs
ranked behind newspapers....

II.

The locomotive fortresses a chocolate gent—
with drumming shoes,
emotive like silver.
A cardboard suitcase—
theatre of his *Power*—
enshrines cologne
splashed from accomplished bottles.

He hunkers down,
bunks with folk roots,
only rising to achieve
the podium of each station.

Serving you,
he might look *Servile*?

Nope! He's putting money in his *Bourse*.
(His improbable salary counts on pennies.)

His *Aesthetics* are military,
militant.
His *Art* wrecks *Artifice*.

His comings-and-goings revamp
neighbourhoods, cities, nations....

No awkward breeding on his part!
No diffident blarney on his lips!

The tinsel rain of his shower
turns to talcum powder snow.

His diamond tie-clip could summon tears.

His alligator shoes slide, snapping up light.

His tony cutlery jazzes up a place.

Ringed, his fingers be semaphore signals,
buttressed by cufflinks—
a gold watch—
a gold chain hooking his vest pocket,
just under his pinstripe jacket.

He knows that "*Adequate* ain't *Perfect*"—
so he keeps whiskey close by,
as emergency polish;
buffs buttons that are little, brass suns.

A black-tie man,
Caesar of *The Bloody Caesar*
(nailed just right),

his pipe bowl smoking—

his top hat always ready to replace
his de facto *képi*.

His *Pedagogy*? *Theology*!
"I can't be God, but neither can you:
so, we both just best be good!"

His medals are gold leaves.

Time and time again,
he figures he's just gotta go on and on and on;

Survival's his birthright:
Arrival's his right.

History is timeless *Relevance*.

His words urge *Emancipation*;
his gestures ignite illumination:
See white gloves and a matchstick aflame.

His shoes, chafing carpet—
or worrying linoleum—
transport remedies;
his passengers swap cigarette smoke.

He scours slop; he purges *Disease*;
He corrects whatever's crooked or untidy.
He bids you relax
in unavoidable *Purity*—
that parity with *Luxury*.

The train gobbles up track, leaves behind stops.

The locomotive courses fiery,
through gloom,
or dazzle—
flickering,
as its wheels dicker.

Your porter remembers sibilant, church sermons—
the persuasive hallelujahs,
the unforgettable, exhilarating cries—

like a jazz combo tuning up.

Arriving, crossing that bridge,
he sees Toronto swing into view,
jittering,
Cubist, already jumping—

like Josephine Baker in Pigalle!

Time for a night on the town:
Silk shirt, wool pants, leather coat;
to see a lady with lips like roses,
eyes like carnations,
her whole face a bouquet.

To set out Champagne, flutes,
spy faces slender and tender, gilded, therein,
those percolating bubbles,
while necking in moonlight,
savouring macaroon-tasty,
maroon-tinted kisses—

such homemade ambrosia....

    iii.

Back on deck, aboard the locomotive,
fording the ravines, the chasms, the streets,

auspicious singing of steel wheels—

bound for Ottawa, Montreal, New York City,
Windsor, Winnipeg—

Toronto becomes a receding triumph,
lights bedraggled by the gauze of *Memory*,
or the tears of *Nostalgia*....

And those bridges traversed—
pig-iron forged into core-10 steel—

help you pull your weight—
your freight—

of *Troubles*, *Solutions*,
and *Resolutions*—

to *Improvement* upon *Improvement*,
sudden as personal *Resurrection*.

Train Conversation

There were two people unwinding in that room.
Three people wounding guitars.

A sip of vodka, a little rum, some beer,
And it's "Blah! Blah! Blah!" And shit all over.

I was getting pissed but there's no ex-boyfriend refund.
Dance with him once and you love him forever.

We watched wrestling and tried the moves on each other.
I'm talking women's rights!

The most popular, green-eyed blonde of the Miramichi
Aced every exam. She was, like, there. Moaning.

I understand why she's a bitch now.
She didn't molest him when she could.

(Girls like that, they get laid, and say,
"Fuck off! You's ugly.")

But who says you have to wake up to "Red, Red Wine"
Every morning? Snow infiltrating tarpaper.

Yikes! That sucks!
But why must she carry her dildo everywhere?

I'm really very interestingly broke.
But I've got dark, blondish-brown hair.

(The Holy Family was clearly from Palestine-Israel.
They had dark skin, black hair, and brown eyes.)

124 I'll go out clubbing tonight too. Who knows?
"Out of all this *Beauty*, sumpin must come."*

---

* Cf. Pound.

Toronto Tantra

Up from the hushed whoosh of subway doors
parting

to trace dawn's rosy circumstance,

see Lake Ontario coast *Tkaronto*—
where "trees stump in water"—
yield a golden edge—

as fiery as sunlit trolley tracks.

I look up
at either the uncontrollable grace of branches
or at the undeniable gilt of bank windows,

those skyscrapers whose tips
dissect clouds,

and I know unaccustomed *Rapture*,
the blissful *Seizure*.

    *

Breathing is optimistic work—
for we hanker to do great things....

Downtown, I pass a construction site—
a vortex of hammers—
unbridled gaiety of clanging, banging,
chiming, clamours—
so girders struggle to square
an elongated rectangle,
inching upward,

toward *Glamour*—
where metal and glass start to look like light.

126 Stop at the base of this *formato loco*—
or "formed space"—
watch pale matter,
fervent grey,
pour out in magisterial sums—
gallons that must weigh tons—
once cement grades to concrete.

The labourers look chestnut-coloured—
incomparably Italian
(as Neapolitan as Naples),
or uncompromisingly Jamaican,
their *patois* thickened into silver oratory,
an oral graffiti—
or Creole fiesta—
that is *Poetry* undistilled.
Or the workers are Finns—
guys who make red brick
look like cedar slats.

(Finland is to stone
what Italy is to wine
and Jamaica is to song.)

Each nationality is mouthfuls of accents—
as cosmopolitan as the cosmos.

It is Toronto's *modus vivendi*,
right?

To compose a Commonwealth
courageously gorgeous

where every citizen conspires
like jazz musicians,
improvising
Beauty.

    *

Passing comparable
edifices, marble,
but phosphorescent as mint ice cream,
and streetcars—
those unfrivolous, whirring engines—
I stride pavement
bright with light and strident with shade—
so my high-noon stroll
unfurls like fingers prancing piano keys,
and I move in a jazz razzmatazz,
unto Kensington Market
and Chinatown,

dreamy, perfumed shops,

as global as a belly,

where tourists ignite a storm cloud
of camera flashes

and neon signs glare with crayon pugnacity
in nagging contradiction:

top-dollars for gold,
rock-bottom prices for all else.

    *

A city is an exact civilization,
but still is as flexible as a jungle:

That's Toronto—
"land of plenty"
(in the Native tongue)—
where electricity, detesting dust,
bonds citizens in ligatures of light—
what's indestructible as diamonds.

Our accents are either sugar-frosted
or extra salty, extra spicy,
and always voicing appropriate heat.

A local-coloured water-colourist,
I delineate Toronto's Great Lakes coastal spectrum—
its alternative rainbow
of cyanotype skies,
cinematic sun amid cinnamon dusk,
lemon-tinted maples,

so all delusions of *Modesty* end

and Toronto beams

a down-to-earth North Star

with poets as sincere
as the Real McCoy.

À Guerino Capobianco (1925–2007) [*First Take*]

For Pier Giorgio Di Cicco, Poet Laureate of Toronto, 2005–09

Mason, carpenter, cement layer, vintner,
East York neighbour,
scintillant exile of Sicily:

You'd lounge briefly, take a snoozing smoke,
a snack of a puff,
while huddling in your garage,
out of reach of rain.

Or you'd make a stove shed the warmth of a church.

Or you'd tune your radio, dredging up
nostalgic froth,
some Elvis tune reborn in Sicilian,
while grinning at the beauty of calendar pin-ups
from fifty years ago.

Neighbour, thanks to you, there was a smell of mint leaves
along the back fence,
the must of wine from grapevine leaves
wafting from your backyard,
a grafting of Monteleone, Sicilia, replanted in East York.
Your garden was *Poetry* gone green.

Yet, you, *beau citoyen*, you looked dowdy,
run-down, unpoetical, Sally-Ann-shabby,
because labour—doing—was your craft.

You were too busy to look business-like!
How could you indulge the haberdasher
when pay demanded that you get dirty
to make the sidewalks pretty?

You were astonishingly original, Old-World skinny,
a lean artisan,
whose polished cement
never cracked.

If your plaid jacket and work shirt,
work pants and shoes,
seemed otherworldly,
some gritty style,
what of it?
You were an earthy bar of gold—
just as solid and just as gleaming.

Besides, your creed was spelled out
in nine words that suit an immigrant:
"Put money in the bank—
or in a roof."

(Don't waste cash on your gut
or for dressing your back.)

You had ceremonial sulks—
finicky, moody spats—
with hydro clerks and call-centres
because, you complained, "In Canada (America),
everything costs expensive money!"
How you loathed that unpleasant arithmetic.

But, neighbour, how neighbourly you were:
Simple, simpatico.

You could jet volcanic insults,
unknown in English,

at those whose gardens tangled with your own.
But you'd smile with happy exasperation
at my well-schooled idiocy
in tending my sunflowers and peach tree.

Daily, nightly, you'd plod along like a snowplough in a blizzard,
never showing the stern loneliness of old men—
no cranky shyness—
and never hesitating to put paint on whatever was failing,
to shore it up,
spruce it up,
to outlast one more winter, one more decade.

Never any rust or useless dust about you—
or your premises:
all broken things got fixed up
briskly.
You liked nothing half-ass,
no mediocre rigs.

No claptrap, no rigmarole.

There was ministry in your hands—
to squash and mash grapes
to mint wine with a dashing gleam,
or to rustle recalcitrant bushes
so that rose petals open like robins' wings.

The city stands because you have its back.

"To see as the sun sees":
That's the sense of Ecclesiastes—
to know that one life

says everything about life—
from fumbling start to festival
to funeral.

Now, this infernal dawn,
your cigarettes lay useless,
sweet maker of Sicilian songs
and drinker of Niagara wine,
you pass into your measure of Eden—
the earth, a self-contained garden—
without any rococo fuss,
no prolonged civilities.

Your hearse parades you one last time,
down our street, past our houses,
and we doff our hats, bow, wipe off tears—
because a humble saint is gone,
one who brought us honey—
in his beautiful drafting,
of the very concrete that bears us up.

He is lost to us now, for he has run off,
glittering,
to move among sun-faced stars.

*Terza Rima for Revell**

These twin skyscraper cocoons seem a flute
Sliced wide open to show how wind makes song,
Harmonious, though throats and lungs dispute;

Or they're two concaves that never veer wrong,
Rounding each other in a yin and yang,
Bauhaus curvaceous: Each arc gets along—

Liked cupped ears 'netting' stereophonic slang,
Or two cupped hands lifted in *Devotion*,
In supple coddling of *Hope*, where stars gang.

These silver-fleshed 'Horseshoe Falls'—an ocean,
Like Niagara, but sculpted, frozen light,
Everlasting glistening, are *Motion*

Made mellifluous, blueprints allowed flight—
The *modernismo* mojo of T.O.—
Space Age design, a planted satellite.

Thanks to that suave, ingenious Finn—Viljo
Revell, resurrecting *Beauty* in glass,
Steel, and concrete—and no glitch, nothing 'for show,'

Nothing boastful, tawdry, but a Palace
Of Democracy, thus *kulta* (Finnish
For *golden*)—*vox populi veritas*.

Revell refreshed *Architecture*'s finish—
To be stately, but graceful, like France's
Eiffel Tower, and never diminish.

---

* Viljo Revell (1910–64).

(See the Taj Mahal.) His plan entrances:
Here's a people's cathedral—insolent,
Twice an 'Arc de Triomphe' the wind dances—

An 'Empire State Building' of government—
An upright amphitheatre, indiscreet—
A splendid, noisy, breathing Parliament,

Where multiple solitudes "kiss and meet,"*
For fifty years, making dreams concrete,
Via laws most strong when they are most sweet.

---

* Cf. Rainer Maria Rilke.

The Peacock's Throne

Toronto, May-June 2015

Invigorating news!
A rebel inmate has escaped
the High Park Zoo
and gone recklessly on the lam!

Yet, who can fence in *Majesty*?
Who can imprison a cathedral?
Who can lock up *Dreaming*?
What bureaucrat can cage the sun?

There's something Persian about a peacock,
versifying Omar Khayyam,
to be at large, "crooning in the wilderness,"
strutting a stained-glass fan,

making its Peacock Throne the very sky
under petals of clouds,
to act petulantly *Exquisite*,
in its exorbitant orbit!

But *Radiance* is disobedient, eh?
Prized, unexcelled *Beauty*
is always extravagantly radiant,
an exuberant flaunting

of glittering *Dazzle*—
razzmatazz, phantasmagoria,
as brazen as paisley,
disrupting the prison of *Routine*,

the regimen of *Business-as-usual*,
the dullness and nullity of the *Pedestrian*.
That free-ranging, wandering peacock,
making his throne

your roof, your backyard, your street's maple,
reminds you your habitat
doesn't have to be a self-made cell,
but a castle of emancipated *Imagination*,

as wide-open as the sky.
The escapee peacock proves
Beauty is freedom and *Freedom* beautiful,
prohibiting *Inhibition*.

Bland folderol, civic politics is
Scandals, fireworks, potholes, *Taxes*—
and we accept being trapped
in what's humdrum and/or tedious,

and never tapping into *Rapture*.
Then, that peacock flew free,
reclaimed its true throne, the sky,
signalling that *Beauty* demands *Liberty*,

that *Beauty* simply takes liberties,
that the real art of *Democracy*
is to have us uplift our wings—
dreaming first, then soaring.

GOLD MEDAL

He who has gold is beloved, though he be a dog, and the son of a dog.
HERBERT VIVIAN, *TUNISIA AND THE MODERN BARBARY PIRATES*

Saviours R Us
NYC, JUNE 2015

Wisdom

    We pass—as we like. Unsurpassed graveyards
Expect us—just like our mothers once did.
Without respect, we tire, retire; our breaths
Soon date, expire. We staff our epitaphs.
    As scripted, we find the stars cool to ash,
The sun drops, blood red, into black sackcloth,
And all the wind knows how to do is cry.
How without *Solace* is soulless flesh....
    Grief wells up, washes out our hearts, but tears
Pass away—just as shallow as shadows.
Eventually, we all bed with lilies.
    All *Hope* is privately cruel. *Suffering*
Demands evangelical verve, moxy.
Something renders our desires fraudulent.

Draft

I pencil these lines
as if lighting a mist:

Each letter stands crisp—
at first sight.

But the words falter,
turn cold quicksilver,
mercurial, tinny—
perfectly defective....

All I write erects shifting shadows
or velvet vapours.

In days to come,
I'll not exist—
having retired from constant

drafts....

(*Oblivion* dwarfs obituaries;
parades worms, flies, and cemeteries.)

I will take another glass of wine,
put away the ink,
and sleep, more-or-less happy.

GOLD RECORD

When the thing was done
You clothed me in a robe of woven gold....
PERCY BYSSHE SHELLEY, *THE CENCI*

Unplugged Gypsy King
MALAGA, OCTOBER 2012

Notes

COMMISSIONS/OCCASIONS: "Duplicity" was commissioned by The Art Gallery of Ontario in Winter 2014 to accompany an exhibit, "Portraits of Poets," that opened on April 16, 2014. ¶ "Introduction: *On Paths Known to No One*" opens Cosma's eponymous book (Somerville, MA: Cervena Barva, 2012). ¶ "Upon Reading Flavia Cosma's *Thus Spoke the Sea*" introduces Cosma's eponymous book, (Toronto: KCLF-21, 2008). ¶ "'When He Was Free and Young and Used to Wear Silks': Subtext" was penned for "A Celebration of Austin Clarke," at the International Festival of Authors, Toronto, ON, November 1, 2015. It was written on Halloween 2015 on the train from Montreal (QC) to Toronto (ON), and is derived from key words in Clarke's psychedelic, 1971 short story. ¶ "Spying Mitic's (Bulletproof) 'Kennedy'" was commissioned for the book, *Art or War: Bullet Paintings by Viktor Mitic* (Toronto: Tightrope, 2010). ¶ "A Draft Elegy for B.A. (Rocky) Jones" occupied the front page of *The Novascotian* magazine insert in *The Chronicle-Herald* [Halifax, NS], on November 2, 2013. Happy that the newspaper allowed poetry such prominence, I regret the occasion, which was the passing of Africadia's greatest leader of the last century, namely, Burnley Allen "Rocky" Jones (1941–2013). ¶ "In Homage to Garry Thomas Morse" was penned for *The Globe and Mail*'s video site at its web page. The video was recorded in late January 2016. ¶ "Principles of Good Governance" was my politic response to the sidereal, globally broadcast gossip regarding Toronto's 64th mayor in 2013–14. Recited before Toronto City Council on April 1, 2014, it appeared in *The Toronto Star* on Sunday, April 6, 2014. ¶ "Desolazione Cosmica" was published in *African Writing Online* (Oct/Nov 2007). ¶ "January Trees, or A Civil Elegy" was commissioned by *The Toronto Star* in January 2013 and appeared in the edition of January 27, 2013. ¶ "Early Spring in the Annapolis Royal Historic Gardens" was penned in March 2014 in Annapolis Royal (NS) for the essay collection, *Each Book a Drum: 10 Years of Halifax Humanities* (Halifax, NS: The Halifax Humanities Society, 2015). ¶ "Reverie of The Commons" was written in June 2013, in Helsinki, Finland, for the anthology, *Writing the Common: Poetry Commemorating the 250th Anniversary of the Halifax Common, 1763–2013*, edited by Friends of the Halifax Common (Kentville, NS: Friends of the Halifax Common and Gaspereau Press, 2013). ¶ "Green / Light: A Chronicle of Sun" was commissioned by Toronto Parks and Trees Foundation for its benefit event of June 24, 2013, held at Koerner Hall Galleria, Royal Conservatory of Music, Toronto, ON. The poem featured in the occasion's brochure, *Green Tie 2013*. ¶ "Bridge Crossing" was commissioned for the book, *On Toronto Train Bridges*, authored by Edward Brown, with photos by David McLeod (Toronto: Brown & McLeod, 2015). It was written aboard a VIA Rail train, Toronto (ON) to Ottawa (ON), in May 2015. ¶ "Train Conversation" appeared in *Prism*, 43:2 (Winter 2005). 99% of the lines originate from commentaries overheard while I was aboard a VIA Rail Train, bounding from Toronto to Ottawa, in early January 1999. ¶ "Toronto Tantra" was commissioned by the Toronto Waterfront Revitalization Corporation for performance at the Intelligent Communities Forum 2013, which rolled out at the Polytechnical Institute at New York University, in Brooklyn, NY, on June 6, 2013. ¶ "À Guerino Capobianco (1925–2007) [First Take]" was written in Playa del Carmen, Mexico, in December 2007. However, this elegy for my once-next-door neighbour was presented in rhyming form (i.e. the "[Second Take]") to Toronto City Council in April 2013 and published as such in the Italian-Canadian magazine, *Accenti*, 29 (Spring 2013). ¶ Commissioned for the 50th Anniversary of the opening of Toronto's City Hall towers, "*Terza Rima* for Revell" was written *en route* by train from Montreal (QC) to Toronto (ON), on September 12, 2015, and recited at Nathan Phillips Square the next day. ¶ After a peacock escaped from High Park Zoo, becoming a feel-good story for several days, late May to early June, 2015, CBC Radio Toronto commissioned, "The Peacock's Throne." ¶ "Wisdom" belongs to *Maple Tree Literary Supplement*, 13 (September-December 2012), www.mtls.ca.

MONGREL DETAILS: "Golden Moments" is slang for *orgasm*. The poem was written aboard AC 1915, BCN-YYZ, on 21/12/15. Cross-reference with the litanies in *Blue* (2001), *Black* (2006), and *Red* (2011); see, respectively, "I.i," "IV.iii," and "Other Angles." ¶ "Year of the Fire-Red Monkey" is my response to Taeho Han's "Year of the Red Monkey." ¶ "Pushkin" is attempted rhyme. ¶ "Hearing Peter Stein" is based on a lecture that the opera conductor gave at the University of Toronto on November 28, 2007. ¶ "Reading Pierre DesRuisseaux" was my instant response to the news of the passing of Canada's 4th Parliamentary Poet Laureate, the Québécois poet, Pierre DesRuisseaux (1945–2016). ¶ "*How Europe Underdeveloped Africa*" is a reworking of Walter Rodney's seminal 1972 study. I wrote the poem in Salvador, Brazil, in November 2007, just after three thugs (one black, one brown, one white) mugged me on a rocky beach near my hotel. The original book is likely cursed: A bomb in his car assassinated Rodney in June 1980. My poem was published in *Kola*, 24.2 (Fall 2012). ¶ "Letter from Zanzibar" was written in Zanzibar, Tanzania, in February 2008, but edited in Nantes, France, one year later. ¶ "Venus: An Anatomy" is a blues poem. ¶ "On Reading *Teacher's Pets* by Crystal Hurdle" responds to the B.C. poet's 2014 verse narrative. ¶ "La philosophie dans le boudoir" (1795) is a title from Sade, but uncannily appropriate for the strange, mutual lust between the metaphysically Fascist-hugging Heidegger and the literally Nazi-loving Arendt. ¶ "Abandonment" was written in London, England, in January 2012. It came out in *Trinity University Review* [Trinity College, University of Toronto], CXXIV (Spring 2012). ¶ "Mariangela and the Seduction," "You Die of It," "Grotesque Ravishing," "Gothic Dramas," and "Melancholy Serenity" are all compositions by Ennio Morricone. "Cosmic

Desolation" is a piece by Angelo Francesco Lavagnino. "Love in Flower" is a work by Piero Piccioni. I thank Linda Hutcheon for the English translations of the song titles. Incidentally, these pieces echo the bravura eroticism of classical Roman letters—due to two volumes of Martial that I purchased in Istanbul in 2003. Consider these poems, then, as Turkish delights. ¶ "Oreo Blues" was written aboard AC 1915, BCN-YYZ, on 21/12/15. ¶ *"Editoriale"* was written in Bellagio, Italy, in October 1998. ¶ "À Rapallo" was written in Rapallo, Italy, in May 2010. ¶ "Draft" is a last word.

These poems were all composed between 1998 and 2016.

GOLD WATCH

Want gold want gold
Gold of eternity
JACK KEROUAC, "209TH CHORUS"

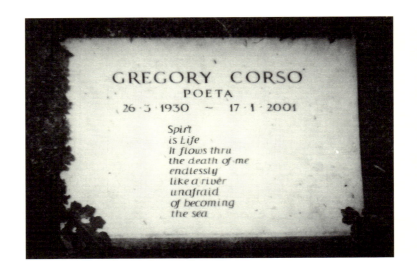

© G[E]C

ROMA, FEBRUARY 2014

Acknowledgements

SURVEYING THE IMAGES (IN ORDER OF APPEARANCE)

Compound Interest Cimitero, Venezia, Italia, Aprile MMX. 149
Hostile Witness Lisbon, Portugal, March MMIX.
The Light Gets In Oswiecim ("Auschwitz"), Poland, May MMXV.
Black Power! Lisbon, Portugal, March MMIX.
The Kiss (of Death) Cimitero, Venezia, Italia, Aprile MMX.
Guess Who's Afraid of V. Woolf! Valletta, Malta, August MMXI.
His Pound of Flesh Cimitero, Venezia, Italia, Aprile MMX.
T-or-ont-au Valletta, Malta, August MMXI.
Saviours R Us NYC, USA, June MMXV.
Unplugged Gypsy King Malaga, Spain, October MMXII.
© G[E]C Roma, Italia, Febraio MMXIV.

All snaps are by the author, save for *Compound Interest*, which is by Riitta Tuohiniemi.

MERCI À TOUS: My "Home Thoughts from Abroad" authorial praxis is indebted to the Rockefeller Foundation's Bellagio Center (Italy) Fellowship (1998); the Pierre Elliott Trudeau Foundation's Fellowship Prize (2005–08); Harvard University's William Lyon Mackenzie King Visiting Professorship in Canadian Studies (2013–14); the Art Gallery of Ontario (2014); and—through every overarching twist and turn and touch-down and tangent—Dr. Sonia Labatt, Ph.D., and Victoria University (*via* The E.J. Pratt Professorship at the University of Toronto). I owe them all; but none bears any responsibility for any errors or immoralities evident here.

Essential editing assistance derives from Ama Ede, *The* John Fraser, Diana Manole, Riitta Tuohiniemi, and Paul Zemokhol. M. Jean Wells-Papenhausen (1942–2012) added zest. Andrew Steeves of Gaspereau Press is a perfect-pitch poet and printer, and his felicities heighten pleasures throughout.

150 The poems were edited in Helsinki (Finland); Funchal, Madeira (Portugal); aboard AC 1915, BCN-YYZ (on December 21, 2015); Hull (Québec); Miami Beach (Florida); Catania (Sicily); and Toronto (Ontario) between October 2015 and April 2016.

GOLD RUSH

You know what gold is these days?
You know where it's goin'?
RICHARD ROTHSTEIN, *DEATH VALLEY*

An Alphabetic List of Poem Titles

Abandonment, 88
A Draft Elegy for B.A. (Rocky) Jones, 60
À Guerino Capobianco (1925–2007) [First Take], 129
"Amore In Fiore", 91
À Rapallo, 113
Austin C. Clarke's "When He Was Free and Young and He Used to Wear Silks" (1971): Subtext, 32
Bridge Crossing, 117
"Desolazione Cosmica", 81
"Drammi Gotici", 84
Draft, 140
Duplicity, 17
Editoriale, 92
Early Spring in the Annapolis Royal Historic Gardens, 98
Golden Moments, 18
Green/Light: A Chronicle of Sun, 107
Hearing Peter Stein, 45
"How Europe Underdeveloped Africa", 51
In Homage to Garry Thomas Morse, 66
Introduction: *On Paths Known to No One*, 27
January Trees, or A Civil Elegy, 95
"La philosophie dans le boudoir", 79
"Lei Se Ne Muore", 82
Letter from Zanzibar, 53
"Malinconica Serenità", 90
"Mariangela E La Seduzione", 80
On Reading *Teacher's Pets* by Crystal Hurdle, 78
Oreo Blues, 86
Peacock's Throne, The, 135
Principles of Good Governance, 69
Pushkin, 44
"Rapimento Grottesco", 83
Reading Pierre DesRuisseaux, 47
Reverie of The Commons, 103
Spying Mitic's (Bulletproof) *"Kennedy"*, 56
Terza Rima for Revell, 133
Toronto Tantra, 125
Train Conversation, 123
Upon Reading Flavia Cosma's *Thus Spoke the Sea*, 28
Venus: An Anatomy, 77
Welcoming The Year of the Fire-Red Monkey, 20
Wisdom, 139

THIS BOOK WAS SET IN ROD MCDONALD'S
LAURENTIAN TYPES WITH PATRICK GRIFFIN'S
MEMORIAM PRO HEADLINE ASSISTING
ON THE JACKET AND TITLE PAGE

Typographic design by
Andrew Steeves

⤳

Copyright © George Elliott Clarke, 2016

All rights reserved. No part of this publication may be reproduced in any form without the prior written consent of the publisher. Any requests for the photocopying of any part of this book should be directed in writing to Access Copyright: The Canadian Copyright Licensing Agency. ¶ This project was funded, in part, by the Government of Canada (Financé par le gouvernement du Canada) through the Canada Council for the Arts and the Canada Book Fund, and in partnership with the Province of Nova Scotia. ¶ This book was designed and typeset by Andrew Steeves and printed offset and bound under the direction of Gary Dunfield at Gaspereau Press.

1 2 3 4 5 6 7

LIBRARY & ARCHIVES CANADA CATALOGUING IN PUBLICATION

Clarke, George Elliott, 1960–, author
Gold / George Elliott Clarke.

Poems.
ISBN 978-1-55447-157-7 (paperback)

I. Title.

PS8555.L3748G64 2016   C811'.54   C2016-902186-6

GASPEREAU PRESS LIMITED ¶ GARY DUNFIELD & ANDREW STEEVES ¶ PRINTERS & PUBLISHERS
47 CHURCH AVENUE, KENTVILLE, NOVA SCOTIA B4N 2M7
Literary Outfitters & Cultural Wilderness Guides